Sugar Rymmed Potions and Pastries Presents:

Shot GIRL Summer

Sugar Rymmed Potions and Pastries Presents:

Shot Girl Summer

This recipe book is for those who want to make a unique, delicious drink, any time of the year (especially summertime), year after year, as a home-tender. Whether you're a kick-back-tender, a girl's night in-tender, or an end-of-the-week-tender, you can follow this book to wow your guests and impress yourself. Whichever type of tender you are, you don't have to be a certified bartender (like me *wink*) to make a good drink. With these simplified and easy-to-follow instructions, you'll be able to create your libations without the complication of mixology/bartending jargon, multiple utensils, hard-to-find ingredients, and fancy processes. We won't even have to use measurement tools! Best of all, the ingredients I've chosen are great quality with mid-stream pricing.

Making beautiful drinks has never been so simple!

Here are a few tips before starting:

Read each step to see all ingredients needed before beginning to pour.

- In this book, pouring amounts are "measured" in counts (per second). When pouring, tip the bottle so the stream pours no greater than the size of your pinky finger. If your pours are consistent, the ratio will be good. If you want to get a pour spout for your bottles, you can. If you mistakenly pour out too much liquor, make sure you make up with it by leveling out the chaser/mix-ins.

- Some recipes call for simple syrup (which you could buy). It's easy to make: Add 1-part warm water to 1-part sugar and stir or shake until it's fully integrated.

- Having crushed ice is great, but any type of ice works fine. Add ice in the glasses to your taste, but ALL these drinks need to have ice in them to dilute the drink properly, unless it's a shot. You can chill the shot glasses in the freezer ahead of time.

- You can use any type of glass. Just make sure it is large enough to hold the liquid involved.

I make my drinks with sugar rims (hence the name). To do so, get a bowl or a plate that are wider than your drink glasses. Rub a lime/lemon wedge around the rim of your glass. Pour sugar in the bowl/plate. Press your glass' rim into the sugar.

In the recipes, I specify the brands that I like to use, but feel free to make substitutions

START WITH A SHOT!

Shot Caller---

Money Shot---

EASE INTO A NICE COCKTAIL

Creeper --

Surely Tempting --

Pineapple Pleasure--

Summer Reign---

Juice Box---

Berry Good-Good--

IT'S TIME TO GO UP!

Going Up! --

On and Popping ---

Meet the Mixologist

START WITH A SHOT!

Shot Caller

This is a quick journey into fruity tequila land.

1. Grab a chilled shot glass (1.5+ oz.)

2. Pour in 2 counts of *1800 Tequila*

3. Pour in 2 counts of *Barefoot Peach Moscato*

4. Drop in the slightest dash of *pineapple juice*

5. Drop in a *stemmed maraschino cherry* from the jar and don't be afraid to let a bit of the juice get into the glass

Shots are served! Smize and lick your lips.

Money Shot

This brandy-based shot will have you feeling like money!

1. Grab a chilled shot glass (1.5+ oz.)

2. Pour in 2 counts of *Ciroc French Brandy*

3. Pour in 2 counts of *Oliver Sweet Red Wine*

4. Drop in the slightest dash of *apple juice*

5. Drop in a *stemmed maraschino cherry* from the jar

Shots are served! Eat the cherry and tongue-tie a knot with the stem.

Creeper

This drink is one of my customer faves, which is usually called Tropical Lemonade Colada. But for Shot Girl Summer, we're going to level it up a notch.

1. Grab a "sugar rymmed" glass of 10 or more ounces, maybe a highball glass. Add in a few ice cubes (or crushed).

2. Pour in 4 counts of *Svedka Mango Pineapple vodka*

3. Pour in 4 counts of *Captain Morgan <u>white</u> rum*

4. Pour in 4 counts of *pineapple juice*

5. Pour in 3 counts of *mango mixer*

6. Pour in 5 counts of *Simply Lemonade*

7. Pour in 1 count of *simple syrup*

8. Stir, keeping the spoon against the glass

Garnish with a pineapple

DRINK UP! But don't be a creeper.

Surely Tempting

This is what you call taking a Shirley Temple to another level. If you opt to - leave it virgin but keep the pineapple in!

1. Grab a "sugar rymmed" glass of 10 or more ounces, maybe a tall highball glass. Add in a few ice cubes (or crushed) and several cherries.

2. Pour in 4 counts of *1800 Tequila*

3. Pour in 2 counts of *Malibu Coconut rum*

4. Pour in 5 counts of *Sprite*

5. Pour in 5 counts of *pineapple juice*

6. Stir, keeping the spoon against the glass

7. Pour in 1 count of *grenadine*

Twirl like Shirley and DRINK UP!

Pineapple Pleasure

Do you like pina coladas? Do you like to put the lime in the coconut? Come here.

1. Grab a "sugar rymmed" (or shaved coconut rimmed) glass of 10 or more ounces, maybe a large margarita glass. Add in a few ice cubes (or crushed).

2. Pour in 4 counts of *Captain Morgan white or spiced rum*

3. Pour in 2 counts of *pina colada mixer*

4. Pour in 2 counts of *pineapple juice*

5. Pour in a half and half mix of *lime juice/simple syrup* as needed, at least 1 count

6. Stir, keeping the spoon against the glass, or blend in a blender for a better mixture

Garnish with a pineapple wedge

Summary Reign

Reign /rān/ n. The period in which a king or queen rules.

Well raise one hand if you're the ruler. Use the other hand to pick up your glass. Take a sip and do your "royalty bop". This summer is your time!

1. Grab a "sugar rymmed" glass of 8 or more ounces, maybe a short tumbler. Add in a few ice cubes (or crushed).

2. Pour in 4 counts of *Crown Royal Apple*

3. Pour in 2 counts of *ginger ale*

4. Pour in 2 counts of *Simply Peach*

5. Stir, keeping the spoon against the glass

Garnish with 2 fresh peach slices, if desired

Juice Box

This fruity drink is a perfect mix of sweet and tangy. Even without the liquor, it's likely to be your favorite juice.

Before making the drink* Get 8 blackberries and smush them. Put the berry smush in a saucepan with ¼ cup of sugar and a squeeze of lemon. Heat on medium-high heat while constantly stirring. Once berries cook down and forms a syrupy consistency, pour over a strainer into an extra cup, pressing out all of juice from the berries into the strainer with spoon. Sit this to the side and let it cool.

1. Grab a "sugar rymmed" glass of 10 or more ounces, maybe a large margarita glass. Add in a few ice cubes (or crushed) and a few black berries.

2. Pour in the *blackberry syrup*

3. Pour in 3 counts of *Jose Cuervo tequila*

4. Pour in 2 counts of *Blue Curacao*

5. Pour in 8 counts of *Simply Limeade*

6. Squeeze in a half slice of large *lemon*

7. Stir, keeping the spoon against the glass

8. Pour in 1 count of *grenadine*

Garnish with a slice of lime and a cherry

This is your juice box. Keep your juice box WET!

Berry Good-Good

When you say something is "that good-good", keep this drink on your mind. In fact, after having this drink, that's how you should refer to it with your lovers and friends.

Ex) "Anybody want some of that good-good???"

Try it for yourself.

1. Grab a "sugar rymmed" glass of 10 or more ounces, maybe a highball glass. Add in a few ice cubes (or crushed). Dice 3 strawberries and smush them at the bottom of the glass with a spoon.

2. Pour in 4 counts of *Tito's vodka OR Hennessy cognac*

3. Pour in 1 count of *strawberry mixer*

4. Pour in 4 counts of *Simply Lemonade*

5. Pour in 1 count of *simple honey (replace sugar with honey in simple syrup)*

6. Stir, keeping the spoon against the glass

Garnish with a fresh mint leaf for a pretty aesthetic

IT'S TIME TO GO UP!

Going Up

You've been waiting on a moment to let loose and alert your D.D. This is your moment! GOING UP!

1. Grab a "sugar rymmed" glass of 10 or more ounces, maybe a large margarita glass. Add in a few ice cubes (or crushed).

2. Pour in 2 counts of *Tito's vodka*

3. Pour in 2 counts of *Seagram's gin*

4. Pour in 2 counts of *Captain Morgan <u>white</u> rum*

5. Pour in 2 counts of *Jose Cuervo tequila*

6. Pour in 2 counts of *Gran Marnier*

7. Pour in 1 count of *mango mixer*

8. Pour in 10 counts of Sprite

9. Stir, keeping the spoon against the glass

10. Pour in 2 counts of *Simply Peach*

Garnish with a stemmed cherry and a lemon wedge

On and Popping

his drink is good to get the blood flowing. My advice would be to sip slow and tell a friend to hide your phone from you. No tipsy texting!

1. Grab a "sugar rymmed" glass of 8 or more ounces, maybe a large martini glass. Add in a few ice cubes (or crushed).

2. Pour in 4 counts of *Seagram's gin*

3. Pour in 2 counts of *cranberry juice*

4. Squeeze in the juice from half of a *large orange*

5. Pour in 1 count of *simple syrup*

6. Top it off with a splash of grenadine

7. Stir, keeping the spoon against the glass

8. Pop a bottle of *Cook's champagne* and pour in 2 counts

Garnish with an orange slice and 2 cherries

Meet the Mixologist

Shay T. Danford

Licensed Bartender/Mixologist

Self-Taught Baker/Treat Maker

Florida A&M University Graduate

Jacksonville, Florida Native

@ Sugar_Rymmed on Instagram, Tik Tok and Facebook

SugarRymmedPnP.com

Contact- SugarRymmedPnP@gmail.com

Made in the USA
Columbia, SC
14 March 2023

13762079R00015